ICONS

EGYPT STYLE

EGYPT

Exteriors   Interiors

STYLE
Details

EDITOR **Angelika Taschen**
PHOTOS **Deidi von Schaewen**

TASCHEN
KÖLN LONDON LOS ANGELES MADRID PARIS TOKYO

Front cover: Inside: Zeina Aboukheiri's splendid salon in Luxor
Back cover: Outside: Raouf Mishriki's idyllic pool in Sakkarah

Couverture : Mondes intérieurs : le somptueux salon de Zeina Aboukheir à Louxor
Dos de couverture : Mondes extérieurs : la piscine idyllique de Raouf Mishriki à Sakkara

Umschlagvorderseite: Innenwelten: Der prachtvolle Salon von Zeina Aboukheir in Luxor
Umschlagrückseite: Außenwelten: Am idyllischen Pool von Raouf Mishriki in Sakkarah

Also available from TASCHEN:

Inside Africa
912 pages
3–8228–5771–8

To stay informed about upcoming TASCHEN titles, please request our magazine
at www.taschen.com or write to TASCHEN, Hohenzollernring 53, D-50672 Cologne,
Germany, Fax: +49-221-254919. We will be happy to send you a free copy
of our magazine which is filled with information about all of our books.

© 2005 TASCHEN GmbH
Hohenzollernring 53, D-50672 Köln
www.taschen.com

Concept by Angelika Taschen, Berlin
Layout and general project management by Stephanie Bischoff, Cologne
Texts by Christiane Reiter, Berlin
Lithography by Horst Neuzner, Cologne
English translation by Pauline Cumbers, Frankfurt am Main
French translation by Thérèse Chatelain-Südkamp, Cologne

Printed in Italy
ISBN 3–8228–3911–6

CONTENTS SOMMAIRE INHALT

Unmoved for thousands of years, she stares straight ahead of her out of stony eyes. Despite her broken nose, her ever more porous stone, and the curiosity of her beholders, she certainly puts on a good face, as if for eternity. The sphinx, the animal sculpture with the head of a Pharaoh, symbolizes both the ancient magic and the fascinating aloofness which Egypt radiates. It is a unique monument – in a unique society. On an area of a million square kilometres, the open-air museum that is Egypt gathers together relics of almost seven thousand years of history: the pyramids of Gizeh, the temple of Luxor, and the graves in the Valley of the Kings, to mention just a few. Egypt is regarded as one of the world's oldest travel destinations – even in ancient times, strangers followed the trails of stones, and in the 19th century, a veritable Egypt mania broke out among the European bohème and Thomas Cook despatched the first package-tours to the land of the Nile – always during the "Egyptian season" between December and April. Although all

IN THE LAND OF THE SPHINX

Christiane Reiter

Immobile depuis des millénaires, il regarde fixement devant lui avec ses yeux de pierre. Et malgré son nez perdu, sa roche de plus en plus poreuse et la curiosité des touristes, on sent qu'il restera impassible pour l'éternité. Sculpture d'un lion à tête de pharaon, le sphinx est le symbole de ce charme magnétique et de cette inaccessibilité fascinante qui émanent de l'Egypte depuis les temps ancestraux. Il est un monument exceptionnel dans un pays hors du commun. Car ce musée en plein air qu'est l'Egypte rassemble sur son territoire d'un million de kilomètres carrés les vestiges d'un passé qui compte sept mille ans : les pyramides de Gizeh, le temple de Louxor et les tombeaux de la vallée des Rois n'en sont que quelques exemples. L'Egypte a toujours été une destination priviégiée. Ainsi dans l'Antiquité, les étrangers suivaient déjà les pistes offertes par les pierres ; au XIXᵉ siècle, on assista à une véritable égyptomanie dans les cercles de la Bohème et c'est Thomas Cook qui envoya dans ce pays traversé par le Nil les premiers touristes en voyage organisé et ce, toujours pendant la « saison égyptienne », entre décembre et avril. Si l'Egypte a connu à toutes les époques de

Sie hat sich seit Jahrtausenden nicht bewegt, blickt aus felsigen Augen starr geradeaus und bewahrt ihrer verlorenen Nase, ihres immer poröser werdenden Gesteins und ihrer neugierigen Besucher zum Trotz eine Contenance wie für die Ewigkeit. Die Sphinx, die Tierskulptur mit dem Kopf eines Pharao, ist ein Symbol für den uralten Zauber und die faszinierende Unnahbarkeit, die von Ägypten ausgehen. Sie ist ein einzigartiges Monument – und in einzigartiger Gesellschaft. Denn das Freilichtmuseum Ägypten versammelt auf einem Staatsgebiet von einer Million Quadratkilometern Relikte einer rund siebentausendjährigen Geschichte; die Pyramiden von Gizeh, der Tempel von Luxor und die Gräber im Tal der Könige sind nur wenige davon. Ägypten gilt als eines der ältesten Reiseländer der Welt – schon in der Antike folgten Fremde den Spuren der Steine, im 19. Jahrhundert brach in Kreisen der europäischen Bohème eine wahre Ägyptomanie aus, und Thomas Cook schickte die ersten Pauschalreisenden ins Land am Nil; stets während der „Ägyptischen Saison" zwischen Dezember und April. Kriege, Krisen und Konflikte sind in allen

the epochs in that long history have been marked by wars, crises, and conflicts, Egypt has always maintained its pride and its reputation as the cradle of civilisation. Not that it ever reveals all its secrets to its guests, neither in public nor in private. Many of its houses are built like bulwarks and painted in natural colours so that they seem to blend in with the desert or mountains like stone chameleons; their only openings onto the street are narrow hatches. Whoever is permitted a look behind the façades, discovers enchanting patios, pools bordered by palms, or hidden terraces, and the interiors bear witness to a clear preference for luxurious accessories, hand-woven carpets and painted walls, gold-threaded fabrics and soft cushions, filigree carvings and mosaics of coloured glass. It is worth travelling into the Egyptian interior, as it can help us to better understand its exterior – and to perhaps feel somewhat closer to the sphinx on our next visit.

son histoire des guerres, des crises et des conflits, elle sut conserver toutefois sa fierté et sa réputation de berceau de l'humanité. L'Egypte ne dévoile jamais à ses hôtes tous ses mystères, que ce soit dans la vie publique ou dans le privé. Un grand nombre de ses maisons sont encore construites comme des bastions ; caméléons de pierre, elles semblent se fondre avec le désert ou les montagnes et elles ne s'ouvrent sur la rue que par d'étroites lucarnes. Seul celui qui est admis à regarder derrière les façades peut découvrir des patios enchanteurs, des bassins bordés de palmiers ou des terrasses à l'abri des regards curieux. Et ce n'est qu'en pénétrant à l'intérieur de la maison que l'on s'aperçoit de l'amour des habitants pour les accessoires luxueux, les tapis tissés à la main, les peintures murales, les étoffes brochées en fils d'or, les coussins moelleux, les sculptures sur bois filigranes et les mosaïques de verre coloré. Un voyage dans les intérieurs égyptiens n'est pas une démarche inutile car il aide aussi à mieux comprendre les extérieurs – et peut-être à se sentir un peu plus proche du sphinx lors d'une autre visite.

Epochen nicht ausgeblieben, doch Ägypten hat sich seinen Stolz und seinen Ruf als Wiege der Zivilisation immer bewahrt. Es offenbart Gästen niemals all seine Geheimnisse; weder in der Öffentlichkeit noch im Privaten. Viele seiner Häuser sind noch wie Bollwerke gebaut, scheinen dank ihrer Naturfarben wie steinerne Chamäleons mit der Wüste oder den Bergen zu verschmelzen und öffnen sich zur Straße hin nur mit schmalen Luken. Erst wer hinter die Fassaden blicken darf, entdeckt verwunschene Patios, von Palmen gesäumte Pools oder versteckte Terrassen. Und erst in den Räumen zeigt sich dann eine Vorliebe für luxuriöse Accessoires, für handgewebte Teppiche und bemalte Wände, golddurchwirkte Stoffe und weiche Kissen, filigrane Schnitzereien und Mosaike aus buntem Glas. Die Reise ins Innere von Ägypten lohnt, denn sie hilft auch dabei, das Äußere besser zu begreifen – und sich beim nächsten Besuch der Sphinx vielleicht ein bisschen näher zu fühlen.

"… All around there was nothing but pale sand, a pallid blue sky and the breath of the earth, which became more and more intense under the sun …"

Sabri Moussa, in *Seeds of Corruption*

«… Tout autour il n'y avait que le sable clair, le ciel bleu pâle et le souffle de la terre qui se condensait sous le soleil …»

Sabri Moussa, dans *Délabrement des lieux*

»… Ringsherum gab es nur blassen Sand, einen mattblauen Himmel und die Atemzüge der Erde, die sich unter der Sonne verdichteten …«

Sabri Mussa, in *Saat des Verderbens*

EXTERIORS

Extérieurs Aussichten

10/11 At the foot of the cliff: the Eco-Hotel Siwa Oasis in the Libyan Desert. *Au pied d'une formation rocheuse : l'hôtel écologique Siwa Oasis dans le désert libyque.* Am Fuß der Felsen: Das Öko-Hotel Siwa Oasis in der Libyschen Wüste.

12/13 Starting the day: shortly before breakfast at the Siwa Oasis. *Le début de la journée : juste avant le petit déjeuner dans l'oasis Siwa.* Start in den Tag: Kurz vor dem Frühstück in der Siwa Oasis.

14/15 Steadfast like a Berber village: the Siwa Oasis with palms in the background. *Capable de se défendre comme un village berbère : l'oasis Siwa Oasis devant une palmeraie.* Wehrhaft wie ein Berberdorf: Die Siwa Oasis vor einer Palmenkulisse.

16/17 Reflected in water: idyllic scene at the pool of the Siwa Oasis. *Se reflète dans l'eau : le décor idyllique autour de la piscine de l'oasis Siwa.* Im Wasser gespiegelt: Idyll rund um den Pool der Siwa Oasis.

18/19 Patterns in the sand: the Libyan Desert. *Traces dans le sable : le désert libyque.* Spuren im Sand: Die Libysche Wüste.

20/21 Sea view: a terrace at the Siwa Oasis. *Avec vue sur la mer : une terrasse de l'oasis Siwa.* Mit Seeblick: Eine Terrasse der Siwa Oasis.

22/23 Fantastic formations: rocks around the Siwa Oasis. *Formes fantastiques : rochers autour de l'oasis Siwa.* Fantasievolle Formationen: Felsen rund um die Siwa Oasis.

24/25 Smooth transition: the Siwa Oasis against the white mountain. *Transition imperceptible : l'oasis Siwa devant la montagne blanche.* Unmerklicher Übergang: Die Siwa Oasis vor dem weißen Berg.

26/27 Relaxing: sofas on a patio at the Siwa Oasis. *Invitent à la détente : sofas dans un patio de l'oasis Siwa.* Zum Zurücklehnen: Sofas in einem Patio der Siwa Oasis.

28/29 Sand tones as far as the horizon: walking at the edge of the desert. *Couleurs de sable jusqu'à l'horizon : promenade en bordure du désert.* Sandtöne bis zum Horizont: Spaziergang am Rand der Wüste.

30/31 Under arches: Dar el Baarat House near Luxor. *Sous des arcades : la maison Dar el Baarat près de Louxor.* Unter Bögen: Das Haus Dar el Baarat bei Luxor.

32/33 Gently arched: staircase to the veranda of Dar el Baarat. *Une voûte tout en douceur : entrée de la véranda de Dar el Baarat.* Sanft gewölbt: Aufgang zur Veranda von Dar el Baarat.

34/35 An address for archaeologists: Hotel Marsam in Luxor. *Une bonne adresse pour les archéologues : l'hôtel Marsam à Louxor.* Eine Adresse für Archäologen: Das Hotel Marsam in Luxor.

36/37 Richly decorated façade: Hotel Al Moudira in Luxor. *Façade richement décorée : l'hôtel Al Moudira à Louxor.* Reich verzierte Fassade: Das Hotel Al Moudira in Luxor.

38/39 Splendid portal: in front of Hotel Al Moudira. *Porte somptueuse : devant l'hôtel Al Moudira.* Prachtvolles Portal: Vor dem Hotel Al Moudira.

40/41 Fine symmetry: at the pool of Hotel Al Moudira. *Belle symétrie : la piscine de l'hôtel Al Moudira.* Schöne Symmetrie: Am Pool des Hotels Al Moudira.

42/43 Monumental: stone sculptures between the desert and Lake Nassar. *Monumentales : sculptures de pierre entre le désert et le Lake Nassar.* Monumental: Steinskulpturen zwischen Wüste und Nasser-Stausee.

44/45 Colossal: cliff formations at the Nile. *Gigantesques : formations rocheuses sur la rive du Nil.* Überdimensional: Felsformationen am Ufer des Nils.

46/47 Like a silhouette: evening by the Nile. *Silhouettes : ambiance crépusculaire sur le Nil.* Wie ein Scherenschnitt: Abendstimmung am Nil.

48/49 Trip to the past: the M.S. Kasr Ibrim on the Nasser reservoir. *Voyage dans le passé : le M.S. Kasr Ibrim sur le lac Nasser.* Reise in die Vergangenheit: Die M.S. Kasr Ibrim auf dem Nasser-Stausee.

50/51 A favourite spot: on the deck of the M.S. Kasr Ibrim. *Une place de choix : sur le pont du M.S. Kasr Ibrim.* Lieblingsplatz: An Deck der M.S. Kasr Ibrim.

52/53 Pool under palms: at the home of Hassan Fathi und Titi Gress. *Piscine à l'ombre des palmiers : chez Hassan Fathi et Titi Gress.* Pool unter Palmen: Bei Hassan Fathi und Titi Gress.

54/55 A private paradise: the garden of the artist Hugh Sowden near Cairo. *Un paradis privé : dans le jardin du peintre Hugh Sowden près du Caire.* Ein privates Paradies: Im Garten des Malers Hugh Sowden bei Kairo.

56/57 Outdoor studio: Hugh Sowden's workplace. *Atelier entouré de végétation : le lieu de travail de Hugh Sowden.* Atelier im Grünen: Der Arbeitsplatz von Hugh Sowden.

58/59 Red and round: the tower of Raouf Mishriki's house in Sakkarah. *Rouge et circulaire : la tour de la maison de Raouf Mishriki à Sakkara.* Rot und rund: Der Turm des Hauses von Raouf Mishriki in Sakkarah.

60/61 A magical place: Raouf Mishriki's swimming pool. *Un lieu magique : la piscine de Raouf Mishriki.* Ein magischer Ort: Am Pool von Raouf Mishriki.

62/63 Colonnade: at the home of Raouf Mishriki. *Colonnade : sur la propriété de Raouf Mishriki.* Säulengang: Auf dem Anwesen von Raouf Mishriki.

64/65 Surrounded: the luxuriant veranda of Amr Khalil in Cairo. *Verdoyante : la véranda d'Amr Khalil au Caire.* Eingewachsen: Die Veranda von Amr Khalil in Kairo.

66/67 Radiantly blue: the Nubian settlement Garb Aswan on the banks of the Nile near Aswan. *D'un bleu étincelant : Garb Aswan, la cité des Nubiens, sur les bords du Nil près d'Assouan.* Leuchtend blau: Die Nubier-Siedlung Garb Aswan am Nilufer bei Assuan.

68/69 Broad pattern: a gate in Garb Aswan. *Recouverte de grands motifs : une porte à Garb Aswan.* Großflächig gemustert: Eine Pforte in Garb Aswan.

70/71 Luminous: twilight in Garb Aswan. *Luminosité : le crépuscule à Garb Aswan.* Leuchtkraft: Dämmerung in Garb Aswan.

"… At the side walls were seats, on the floor lay an embroidered mat. Doves and small birds were painted on the ceiling where the lamp hung …"

Naguib Mahfouz, in *Children of the Alley*

«… Le long des murs latéraux se trouvaient des sièges rembourrés, sur le sol il y avait un petit tapis brodé. Le plafond était là où était suspendue la lampe, avec des peintures de pigeons et de petits oiseaux …»

Naguib Mahfouz, dans *Récits de notre quartier*

»… An den Seitenwänden befanden sich Sitzpolster, auf dem Boden lag eine bestickte Matte. Die Decke war dort, wo die Lampe hing, mit Tauben und kleinen Vögeln bemalt …«

Nagib Machfus, in *Die Kinder unseres Viertels*

INTERIORS

Intérieurs Einsichten

78/79 Rustic flair: salon in the Siwa Oasis. *Ambiance rustique : salon dans l'oasis Siwa.* Rustikales Flair: Salon in der Siwa Oasis.

80/81 Surrounded by stone: bedroom in the Siwa Oasis. *Entourée de pierres : chambre dans l'oasis Siwa.* Ganz von Stein umgeben: Schlafzimmer in der Siwa Oasis.

82/83 Set for four: simple dining-room at the Siwa Oasis with walls out of salt blocks. *Pour quatre : salle à manger toute simple dans l'oasis Siwa avec des murs en block du sel.* Für vier: Schlichtes Esszimmer in der Siwa Oasis mit Wänden aus Salzblöcken.

84/85 In the traditional style: guestroom at the Siwa Oasis. *Construite dans le style traditionnel : une chambre d'ami de l'oasis Siwa.* Im traditionellen Stil erbaut: Ein Gästezimmer der Siwa Oasis.

86/87 Filigree handcrafts: hall at the Hotel Al Moudira in Luxor. *Travail manuel filigrane : le hall de l'hôtel Al Moudira à Luxor.* Filigrane Handarbeiten: Halle im Hotel Al Moudira in Luxor.

88/89 Antique furniture: in Zeina Aboukheir's palatial salon in Luxor. *Mobilier ancien : dans le salon aux allures de palais de Zeina Aboukheir à Louxor.* Antikes Mobiliar: Im palastartigen Salon von Zeina Aboukheir in Luxor.

90/91 The splendour of Egypt: artworks in Zeina Aboukheir's house. *Toute la splendeur de l'Egypte : objets d'art dans la maison de Zeina Aboukheir.* Die ganze Pracht Ägyptens: Kunstwerke im Haus von Zeina Aboukheir.

92/93 Under high arches: Zeina Aboukheir's red-and-gold salon. *Sous des arcs vertigineux : dans le salon rouge et or de Zeina Aboukheir.* Unter hohen Bögen: Im rot-goldenen Salon von Zeina Aboukheir.

94/95 Sleeping like royalty: at the Hotel Al Moudira in Luxor. *Dormir comme un roi : l'hôtel Al Moudira à Luxor.* Schlafen wie die Könige: Im Hotel Al Moudira in Luxor.

96/97 Stylish mix: furniture from different epochs at Zeina Aboukheir's home. *Mélange de styles : meubles d'époques différentes ; chez Zeina Aboukheir.* Stilmix: Möbel aus unterschiedlichen Epochen; bei Zeina Aboukheir.

98/99 Syrian frames: paintings in the bar of the Hotel Al Moudira in Luxor. *Cadre syrien : tableau au bar de l'hôtel Al Moudira à Luxor.* Syrischer Bilderrahmen: Gemälde in der Bar des Hotels Al Moudira in Luxor.

100/101 Seventh heaven: Zeina Aboukheir's bed in Luxor. *Au septième ciel : le lit de Zeina Aboukheir à Luxor.* Im siebten Himmel: Das Bett von Zeina Aboukheir in Luxor.

102/103 Daring mix: Amr Khalil's sumptuous salon in Cairo. *Oser les mélanges : le salon richement décoré d'Amr Khalil au Caire.* Mut zum Mix: Der üppig eingerichtete Salon von Amr Khalil in Kairo.

104/105 Spots of colour: Raouf Mishriki's house in Sakkarah. *Des accents de couleur un peu partout : dans la maison de Raouf Mishriki à Sakkara.* Farbakzente überall: Im Haus von Raouf Mishriki in Sakkarah.

106/107 Coloured glass and soft light: resting place at Raouf Mishriki's home. *Verre coloré et lumière douce : coin-repos chez Raouf Mishriki.* Buntes Glas und weiches Licht: Ruheplatz bei Raouf Mishriki.

108/109 Golden gleam: Amr Khalil's dining-table in Cairo. *L'éclat de l'or : à la table d'Amr Khalil au Caire.* Goldener Glanz: An der Tafel von Amr Khalil in Kairo.

110/111 A dream: glamorous room at the Hotel Al Moudira in Luxor. *Pour rêver : chambre glamour à l'hôtel Al Moudira à Louxor.* Zum Träumen: Glamouröses Zimmer im Hotel Al Moudira in Luxor.

112/113 Oriental style: sofa in Murad Grace's house in Gizeh. *D'inspiration orientale : le sofa dans la maison de Murad Grace à Gizeh.* Orientalisch inspiriert: Sofa im Haus von Murad Grace in Gizeh.

114/115 Red and brown accessories: Murad Grace's fireplace. *Accessoires en rouge et marron : autour de la cheminée de Murad Grace.* Accessoires in Rot und Braun: Am Kamin von Murad Grace.

116/117 Tone in tone: Murad Grace's bedroom. *Ton sur ton : dans la chambre de Murad Grace.* Ton in Ton: Im Schlafzimmer von Murad Grace.

118/119 Relaxing under the vaulted ceiling: in Dar el Baarat in Luxor. *Se détendre sous une voûte : dans la maison Dar el Baarat à Louxor.* Entspannen unterm Gewölbe: Im Haus Dar el Baarat in Luxor.

120/121 Homage to Morocco: a table made of zelliges in Dar el Baarat. *Hommage au Maroc : une table en zelliges dans Dar el Baarat.* Hommage an Marrokko: Ein Tisch aus zelliges in Dar el Baarat.

122/123 Like a red throne: sofa from the souk in Dar el Baarat. *Comme un trône rouge : sofa de souk dans Dar el Baarat.* Wie ein roter Thron: Sofa vom Souk in Dar el Baarat.

124/125 Mosquito net and red cushions: guestroom in Dar el Baarat. *Avec moustiquaire et coussins rouges : la chambre d'ami dans Dar el Baarat.* Mit Moskitonetz und roten Kissen: Gästezimmer in Dar el Baarat.

126/127 Tropical flair: Hugh Sowden's house near Cairo. *Ambiance tropicale dans la maison : chez Hugh Sowden dans les environs du Caire.* Tropenflair im Haus: Bei Hugh Sowden in der Nähe von Kairo.

128/129 Colourful prospect: Hugh Sowden's motley collection. *Perspectives multicolores : sympathique bric-à-brac de Hugh Sowden.* Bunte Aussichten: Hugh Sowdens sympathisches Sammelsurium.

130/131 Calm atmosphere: among the Nubians in Garb Aswan on the Nile. *Atmosphère reposante : chez les Nubiens à Garb Aswan sur le Nil.* Beruhigende Stimmung: Bei den Nubiern in Garb Aswan am Nil.

132/133 Useful wall decor: everyday items used by the Nubians. *Décoration murale utile : accessoires du quotidien des Nubiens.* Nützlicher Wandschmuck: Alltags-Accessoires der Nubier.

134/135 Private realm: chest of drawers and bed in a house in Garb Aswan. *Sphère privée : commode et lit dans une maison de Garb Aswan.* Privater Bereich: Kommode und Bett in einem Haus von Garb Aswan.

136/137 Reflections: bedroom with ample storage space. *Reflet dans le miroir : chambre avec nombreuses possibilités de rangement.* Verspiegelt: Schlafzimmer mit viel Stauraum.

138/139 Storage miracle: among the Nubians in Garb Aswan. *Une pièce bien étrange : chez les Nubiens à Garb Aswan.* Raumwunder: Bei den Nubiern in Garb Aswan.

140/141 Brilliant orange: living-room in a house in Garb Aswan. *Orange vif : salle de séjour dans une maison de Garb Aswan.* Leuchtend orange: Wohnraum in einem Haus von Garb Aswan.

"… The flowers on the low inlaid table reiterate the colours of the cushions deco-
rating the divan …"

Ahdaf Soueif, in *The Map of Love*

«… Les fleurs sur la table basse en marqueterie répètent les couleurs des
coussins qui ornent le divan …»

Ahdaf Soueif, dans *La carte de l'amour*

»… Die Blumen auf dem niedrigen Intarsientisch wiederholen die Farben der
Kissen, die den Diwan schmücken …«

Ahdaf Soueif, in *Die Landkarte der Liebe*

CHARMING DETAILS

Détails charmants Charmante Details

النجم الذهبي

لضبط أبواب السيارات

وتركيب الزجاج وعمل جميع المفاتيح

محمول ١٢٣٦٢١٤٧٨

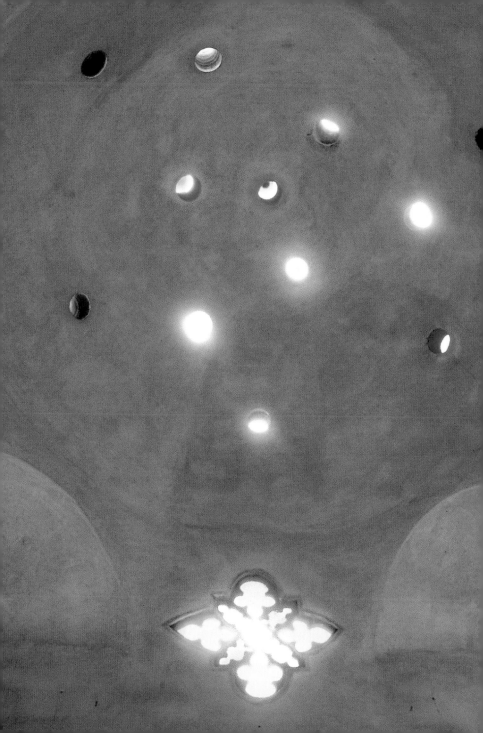

148 Graphic: entrance with patterned frame. *Graphique : entrée de maison encadrée de motifs.* Grafisch: Von Mustern umrahmter Hauseingang.

150 Into the blue: ancient gate. *Regard dans la couleur bleue : porte ancienne.* Blick ins Blaue: Antike Pforte.

151 Like in the old days: the work-a-day. *Comme dans le passé : le travail quotidien.* Wie in alten Zeiten: Arbeitsalltag.

152 Under a sickle moon: door handle decoration. *Sous la demi-lune : poignée de porte décorée.* Unter dem Halbmond: Verzierter Türgriff.

154 In an emergency I: a key maker in Cairo. *Adresse d'urgence I : un serrurier au Caire.* Notfall-Adresse I: Ein Schlüsselmacher in Kairo.

155 In an emergency II: a computer shop in Cairo. *Adresse d'urgence II : un magasin d'ordinateurs au Caire.* Notfall-Adresse II: Ein Computerladen in Kairo.

156 Novelty: shoe-shaped glass lampshade. *Toujours du nouveau : lampe de verre en forme de chaussure.* Laufend Neues: Gläserne Lampe in Schuhform.

158 Colour play: hand-made accessories. *Jeux de couleurs : accessoires fabriqués main.* Farbenspiele: Handgefertigte Accessoires.

159 Shimmering blue tiles: in a Nubian house. *Carreaux aux reflets bleutés : dans une maison des Nubiens.* Blau schimmernde Kacheln: In einem Haus der Nubier.

160 Working with traditional recipes: a servant. *Travailler d'après des recettes de cuisine traditionnelles : un gagiste.* Arbeit nach überlieferten Rezepten: Ein Bediensteter.

162 Entrance: wooden door handle. *Entrée : poignée de porte en bois.* Eingang: Hölzerner Türgriff.

163 View: window with upholstered frame. *Ouverture : fenêtre au cadre rembourré.* Ausblick: Fenster mit gepolstertem Rahmen.

164 Behind the artless curtain: a modern bathroom. *Derrière un rideau naturel : une salle de bains moderne.* Hinter einem natürlichen Vorhang: Modernes Bad.

166 Bamboo panelled: washbasin. *Habillé de bambous : le lavabo.* Mit Bambus verkleidet: Waschbecken.

167 Glittering: evening wear with sequins. *Brille de tous ses feux : habits de soirée avec paillettes.* Glitzernd: Abendgarderobe mit Pailetten.

168 Colour contrasts: dark clay vases on brightly patterned marble slab. *Contrastes de couleurs : Vase en grès foncé sur un plaque de marbre.* Farbkontraste: Dunkle Tonvasen auf hell-gemusterter Marmorplatte.

170 Oven-fresh: traditional flat bread. *Sorti du four : le pain traditionnel.* Frisch aus dem Ofen: Traditionelles Fladenbrot.

171 View of the sky: round construction with open roof. *Regard dans le ciel : construction circulaire au toit ouvert.* Blick in den Himmel: Rundbau mit offenem Dach.

172 King-size: bed at Hotel Al Moudira. *Kingsize : Lit à l'hôtel Al Moudira.* Kingsize: Bett im Hotel Al Moudira.

174 A child's dream: antique rocking horse. *Rêve d'enfant : un ancien cheval à bascule.* Kindertraum: Ein antikes Schaukelpferd.

175 Instead of a starry sky: dome with round coloured windows. *En guise de ciel étoilé : coupole avec fenêtres rondes multicolores.* Statt Sternenhimmel: Kuppel mit bunten Rundfenstern.

176 Under chandeliers: dining hall at the Al Moudira. *Sous le lustre en cristal : salle à manger de l'hôtel Al Moudira.* Unter Kristalllüstern: Speisesaal des Hotels Al Moudira.

178 Door to the inner sanctum: carved wood. *Porte ouvrant sur le saint des saints : battants joliment travaillés.* Tür ins Allerheiligste: Schön geschnitzte Flügel.

179 Cleaning: in front of a highly decorative mirror and bracket. *En plein ménage : devant le miroir richement décoré et la console.* Hausputz: Vor dem reich verzierten Spiegel mit Konsole.

180 Refuge: niche with sofa and filigree window décor. *Pour se dissimuler : niche avec sofa et fenêtre aux décorations filigranes.* Zum Verstecken: Nische mit Sofa und filigranem Fensterschmuck.

182 Antiques: writing-desk, statues, and clay pots. *Antiquités : secrétaire, statues et récipients en grès.* Antiquitäten: Sekretär, Statuen und Tongefäße.

183 A gem: splendidly-decorated window. *Un véritable bijou : fenêtre somptueusement travaillée.* Schmuckstück: Prachtvoll verziertes Fenster.

184 Colourful: blue chest of drawers with gold trimmings. *Des couleurs gaies : commode bleue aux applications dorées.* Farbenfroh: Blaue Kommode mit goldenen Applikationen.

186 Siesta: rocking chair in the shade. *Sieste : rocking-chair à l'ombre.* Siesta: Schaukelstuhl im Schatten.

187 Like in paradise: for an outdoor chat. *Comme au paradis : faire la causette dans la verdure.* Wie im Paradies: Für eine Plauderstunde im Grünen.

Addresses

ADRÈRE AMELLAL DESERT ECO - LODGE
Siwa Oasis
Egypt
Tel. + 20 (2) 736 7879, Fax 735 5489
E-mail: info@eqi.com.eg

HOTEL AL MOUDIRA
Luxor West Bank
Egypt
Tel. + 20 (12) 392 8332, Fax 322 0528
E-mail: moudirahotel@yahoo.com
Website: www.moudira.com

HOTEL MARSAM
Qurna
Luxor West Bank
Egypt
Tel. + 20 (95) 372 403
E-mail: marsam@africamail.com

M.S. KASR IBRIM & M.S. EUGENIE
Lake Nasser
Nubia
Egypt
Tel. + 20 (2) 516 9653, Fax 516 9646
E-mail: eugenie@soficom.com.eg
Website: www.kasribrim.com.eg

The Hotelbook. Great Escapes Africa Shelley-Maree Cassidy / Ed. Angelika Taschen / Hardcover, 400 pp. / € 29.99 / $ 39.99 / £ 19.99 / ¥ 5.900

Inside Africa Ed. Angelika Taschen / Deidi von Schaewen / Hardcover, 2 volumes, 912 pp. / € 99.99 / $ 125 / £ 69.99 / ¥ 15.000

"In two volumes, this is a remarkable, colossal undertaking – more than simply a visual source book." —*House & Garden,* London, on *Inside Africa*

"Buy them all and add some pleasure to your life."

Alchemy & Mysticism
Alexander Roob

All-American Ads 40s
Ed. Jim Heimann

All-American Ads 50s
Ed. Jim Heimann

All-American Ads 60s
Ed. Jim Heimann

Angels
Gilles Néret

Architecture Now!
Ed. Philip Jodidio

Art Now
Eds. Burkhard Riemschneider, Uta Grosenick

Berlin Style
Ed. Angelika Taschen

Chairs
Charlotte & Peter Fiell

Design of the 20th **Century**
Charlotte & Peter Fiell

Design for the 21st **Century**
Charlotte & Peter Fiell

Devils
Gilles Néret

Digital Beauties
Ed. Julius Wiedemann

Robert Doisneau
Ed. Jean-Claude Gautrand

East German Design
Ralf Ulrich / Photos: Ernst Hedler

Egypt Style
Ed. Angelika Taschen

M.C. Escher

Fashion
Ed. The Kyoto Costume Institute

HR Giger
HR Giger

Grand Tour
Harry Seidler, Ed. Peter Gössel

Graphic Design
Ed. Charlotte & Peter Fiell

Havana Style
Ed. Angelika Taschen

Homo Art
Gilles Néret

Hot Rods
Ed. Coco Shinomiya

Hula
Ed. Jim Heimann

India Bazaar
Samantha Harrison, Bari Kumar

Industrial Design
Charlotte & Peter Fiell

Japanese Beauties
Ed. Alex Gross

Kitchen Kitsch
Ed. Jim Heimann

Krazy Kids' Food
Eds. Steve Roden, Dan Goodsell

Las Vegas
Ed. Jim Heimann

Mexicana
Ed. Jim Heimann

Mexico Style
Ed. Angelika Taschen

Morocco Style
Ed. Angelika Taschen

Extra/Ordinary Objects, Vol. I
Ed. Colors Magazine

Extra/Ordinary Objects, Vol. II
Ed. Colors Magazine

Paris Style
Ed. Angelika Taschen

Penguin
Frans Lanting

20th **Century Photography**
Museum Ludwig Cologne

Pin-Ups
Ed. Burkhard Riemschneider

Provence Style
Ed. Angelika Taschen

Pussycats
Gilles Néret

Safari Style
Ed. Angelika Taschen

Seaside Style
Ed. Angelika Taschen

Albertus Seba. Butterflies
Irmgard Müsch

Albertus Seba. Shells & Corals
Irmgard Müsch

Starck
Ed Mae Cooper, Pierre Doze, Elisabeth Laville

Surfing
Ed. Jim Heimann

Sydney Style
Ed. Angelika Taschen

Tattoos
Ed. Henk Schiffmacher

Tiffany
Jacob Baal-Teshuva

Tiki Style
Sven Kirsten

Tuscany Style
Ed. Angelika Taschen

Women Artists
in the 20th and 21st Century
Ed. Uta Grosenick